C000171605

Little Book of
BEADED
CRUSTS
AND
TASSELS

HELEN DAFTER

SALLY MILNER
PUBLISHING

First published in 2008 by
Sally Milner Publishing Pty Ltd
734 Woodville Road
Binda NSW 2583 AUSTRALIA

© Helen Dafter 2008

Design: Anna Warren, Warren Ventures Pty Ltd
Editing: Anne Savage
Photography: Tim Connolly

Printed in China

National Library of Australia Cataloguing-in-Publication data:

Author:	Dafter, Helen.
Title:	Little book of beaded crusts and tassels / Helen Dafter.
Publisher:	Binda, N.S.W. : Sally Milner Publishing, 2008.
ISBN:	9781863513869
Series:	Milner craft series
Subjects:	Tassels.
	Beadwork.
Dewey Number:	746.27

Disclaimer
Information and instructions given in this book are presented in good faith, but no warranty is given nor results guaranteed, nor is freedom from any patent to be inferred. As we have no control over physical conditions surrounding application of information herein contained in this book, the author and publisher disclaim any liability for untoward results.

10 9 8 7 6 5 4 3 2 1

ACKNOWLEDGEMENTS

This little book has been an absolute pleasure to write. For me, creating items with beads is relaxing and allows me to be as creative as I like. I hate counting beads in any great number so the challenge for me over the years has been to design pretty and very decorative beaded objects that require minimal counting. With most of these projects I have succeeded.

My thanks to Sally Milner Publishing for allowing me to step out of the square to create this little book. Thanks also to my family, particularly my husband Glenn, who has put up with beads turning up in all sorts of places and rarely made mention, and also to my regular students who have been supportive and constructive over the years—together we have had some fun times with our individual bead collections.

Contents

Introduction

Crust *n.* a crisp, hard or thick layer or coating that develops on something.

Tassel *n.* a bunch of loose parallel threads that are tied together at one end and used as a decoration.

Add the word 'bead' to the above dictionary definitions and you have a mental image of what these two techniques will create. They can be lots of fun as well, not to mention using up stashes of leftover beads in a very creative manner.

BEAD CRUSTING

This is a term I use to describe covering an object with a sewn layer of a selected bead mix until it is either covered completely or decorated in a specific area. The technique results in a highly decorative effect—and no counting of beads is involved. In many cases the beads do not need to be attached individually and can be sewn onto the desired object in multiples, allowing you to cover an area quite quickly. The instructions for the crusted items show a variety of crusting options.

BEADED TASSELS

All the tassels here are based on a basic beaded tassel construction method— only the beaded drops and the tassel tops vary from the basic tassel. Several versions require minimal counting of beads for the drops, or the repetition of a simple pattern, but generally their construction remains the same. Once the tassel-drop construction techniques are understood, it is possible to vary them to create even more tassels in many different ways.

TOOLS

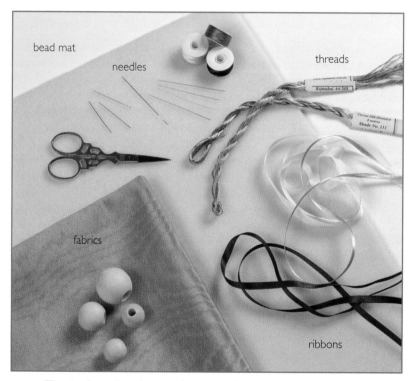

The simple tools and materials required for bead crusting and making beaded tassels

NEEDLES

All crusted items are decorated with sewn beads; no glue is used. The needle you use for a particular piece of crusting should be fine enough to pass through the hole of every bead chosen for that item. It is frustrating if too large a needle is chosen and beads are continuously rejected because it is too large to pass through them. In general a beading needle, which is available in a number of sizes, is ideal. A large-eye beading needle is also available. This has a sharp point at either end with a split in the wire in the middle of the needle, which makes it easy to thread. In many cases the bead crusting mixes are made up of beads which will also allow the passage of a fine straw/milliners needle (size 10) or even a fine crewel needle (size 9). If your beading needle develops a bend, do not despair—it will still be useful—and may make it a little easier to pick up the smaller beads. Needles similar to those used for bead crusting are also suitable for making tassels—always choose a needle which allows smooth passage of the beads to be used to create the tassel drops

THREAD

I always use the specialty beading thread Nymo, which is available in a variety of colours and thread weights. Generally I prefer to use the D size thread in a deep beige colour, which will blend with most coloured beads. I use a black or white beading thread only when I am using white, black or clear beads. In most cases, however, particularly with bead crusting, it is extremely difficult to see the thread so perfect colour coordination of beads and thread is not absolutely critical. Cotton or polyester sewing threads may be used, but there is always a risk that these threads will break and a drop or two of a tassel will be lost.

FABRICS

The fabric you use in the construction of an item may vary—silks, moiré taffetas, fine cottons are all suitable. It is important that the needle passes through the fabric easily, so always test this before starting. If you are making a brooch or a lidded box, similar to those illustrated toward the end of the book, always coordinate the colour of the fabric with the colour of the beads you are using for the crusting.

RIBBONS

Ribbons are specified in the instructions for several of the crusted items, and are used for the loops at the top of the tassels. For most of the crusted tassels, 3 mm double-sided satin ribbon has been used to cover the wooden ball on which the crusting is worked—see page 51.

Silk or satin ribbon is used for the tassel loops. It is important that the ribbon you use will pass easily through the beads you have chosen to create the tassel top. Silk ribbon is finer than satin ribbon, so if the beads for the tassel have very small holes consider using silk in preference to satin.

SCISSORS

Keep a sharp pair of fine embroidery scissors close at hand to cut threads as required. Never allow them to be used for cutting paper or card, as these materials dull the cutting edges and make it difficult to cut the thread.

BEAD MAT

This is a specialty product to place on a table or tray when beading to prevent the beads from rolling. It also makes it easier to pick up beads with the needle, as the beads sit proud of the surface of the bead mat and the needle point does not get caught in the mat.

Bead Basics

bead mixes

spacers

bead caps

Examples of the bead mixes, bead caps and spacers available

BEAD MIXES

These are collections of mixed beads in selected colourways. A mix will include seed beads varying in size from 8 to 12; twisted or plain bugle beads in sizes 1, 2 or 3; pearls up to 3 mm; Miyuku cubes up to 3 mm; triangular beads; second-cut seed beads; and often other beads as well.

Try and keep the size range consistent between the types of beads used in creating a particular item, but vary the finish, mixing translucent, AB (named after the aurora borealis, the bead appearing as if it has been dipped in oil), matt and clear beads. The beads in a bead mix will generally have centre holes.

BEAD CAPS

These are either cast in precious or semiprecious metal, or pressed from metal, and are available in a large range of sizes and finishes. They are designed to fit neatly either side of a specialty or feature bead to enhance its features.

They 'dress up' a bead along a strand and make it appear more important in the sequence.

Remember to choose a bead cap that fits neatly over the end of the bead—not too large or too small.

FEATURE BEADS

These will generally be used at the top of the tassel. Keep in mind the colour of the tassel when selecting feature beads, and choose colours or finishes which further enhance the tassel. A feature bead might be a very decorative metal bead, or a simple glass or acrylic bead enhanced with filigree or cast bead caps.

The size of the holes in feature beads can be critical when they are used as tassel tops. Keep in mind when sourcing beads for this use that the ribbon loop will need to fit through the hole.

SPACERS

Usually made of metal or metallised plastic, these beads can be invaluable in creating interest along the bead strand. A spacer bead can be placed either side of a bead or either side of a bead cap on specialty beads to further enhance the impact of a particular bead. They may be as simple as a small metallic bead or shaped like a flat washer, often with a decorative edge.

SPECIALTY BEADS

These are often an odd shape—leaves, shells, teardrops, flower shapes and so on. Specialty beads are often top-drilled, not centre-drilled, and will require a different threading method if forming part of a tassel. See diagram of threading top-drilled beads on page 15.

Beaded Tassels

CONSTRUCTION BASICS

Ribbon loop

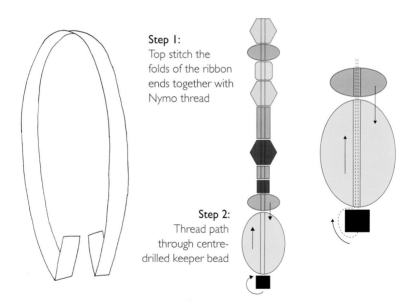

Step 1:
Top stitch the folds of the ribbon ends together with Nymo thread

Step 2:
Thread path through centre-drilled keeper bead

Step 3:
Thread path through beads including keeper bead/s to form tassel drop

Step 4:
Thread the feature beads using a loop of thread to assist in threading them over the ribbon to the top of the tassel drop

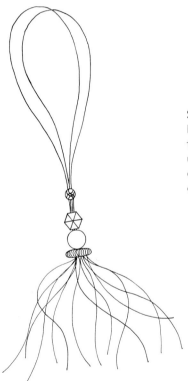

Step 5:
Move top feature bead up to the length of ribbon and glue underneath to prevent it slipping off the ribbon loop. Reposition over small amount of glue.

Notes

* In each of the following sets of instructions the materials listed will make one tassel.

* Nymo beading thread is used for all projects.

* Always ensure you have sufficient thread to return to the ribbon loop and secure before commencing threading the next beaded drop.

* Each beaded drop should begin with the smaller beads from any mix. This will ensure that the top of the drop remains as fine as possible, giving good definition between the tassel top and the feature beads.

$\mathcal{R}$AJMAHAL TASSEL

You will need

20 cm (8 in) 3 mm double-sided satin
    ribbon
6 decorative feature beads, metallic and
    coloured

1 skein Rajmahal art silk thread
Nymo thread
beading needle

ribbon loop

feature beads:
length of bead
4.5 cm (1¾ in)

tassel skirt: length of
threads 9 cm (3½ in)

Method

Remove the paper wraps from the skein of thread. Open the skein out into a circle shape, but leave the ends knotted together. Loop the lengths of thread over your fingers five times and even up these loops by stretching your fingers apart. Use a doubled length of Nymo thread to sew the loops together firmly at the point opposite to where the ends are knotted together. Knot the ends of ribbon together, pulling the knot until it is very tight. Loop the folded end of the ribbon through the loops of thread and back through itself until the knot of the ribbon sits over where the threads are stitched together. Use a short length of thread to pull the ribbon loop through the feature beads to form the tassel top. A bead with a very large centre hole is required to fit the sewn thread loops and the ribbon through the centre hole. A knot in the ribbon or a small amount of PVA or craft glue under the top feature bead will prevent the beads from slipping off the ribbon. Cut the thread loops apart at the base of the tassel and use an old toothbrush to gently tease the threads apart. Steam to straighten.

$\mathcal{L}$OOPED TASSEL

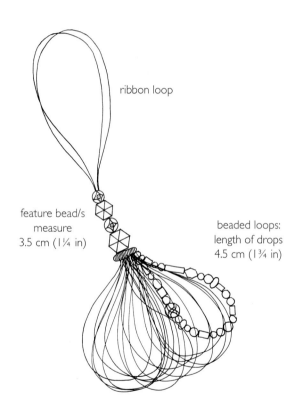

ribbon loop

feature bead/s
measure
3.5 cm (1¼ in)

beaded loops:
length of drops
4.5 cm (1¾ in)

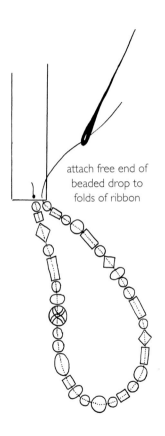

attach free end of
beaded drop to
folds of ribbon

Method

Fold the ends of the ribbon over
about 1 cm (¼ in) from the end
and topstitch the folded edge
together. Using a single strand
of Nymo with a double knot
threaded through the folds at
the base of the ribbon, begin to
randomly thread beads from the
mix until the strand of beads is
8 cm (3 in) long. Take the needle
and thread to the folded base of
the ribbon and stitch to secure,
thus forming a loop of beads.

Repeat this step 16 times.
Use a short length of thread to
pull the ribbon loop through the
feature beads to form the tassel
top. A knot in the ribbon or a
small amount of PVA or craft
glue under the top feature bead
will prevent these beads from
slipping off the ribbon.

$\mathcal{C}$ORAL TASSEL

You will need

20 cm (8 in) 7 mm silk ribbon
5 decorative feature beads, metallic and
    coloured

1 quantity bead mix (30–40 g)
Nymo thread
beading needle

Method

Fold the ends of the ribbon over about 1 cm (¼ in) from the end and topstitch the folded edges together. Using a single strand of Nymo with a double knot threaded through the folds at the base of the ribbon, begin to randomly thread beads from the mix until the strand of beads is 10 cm (4 in) long. Each strand and branch of coral is held in place with a 'keeper' bead— see detail diagram of keeper beads. When the strand is the correct length, and after threading the keeper bead, retrace the thread path approximately one-fifth of the way up the strand and emerge with needle and thread. Pick up about 2 cm (¾ in) of beads from mix, add keeper bead and retrace thread path back to main strand. Repeat to create four branches in total along the strand. When you return to the ribbon, create a slipknot at the base of the ribbon to ensure the drop does not slip.

Create nine more drops similar to this. Then, using the remaining mix, create shorter strands of coral with one or two branches and shorter branch length strands only at the top of the tassel. Fasten thread. Use a short length of thread to pull the ribbon loop through the feature beads to form the tassel top. A knot in the ribbon or a small amount of PVA or craft glue under the top feature bead will prevent the beads from slipping off the ribbon.

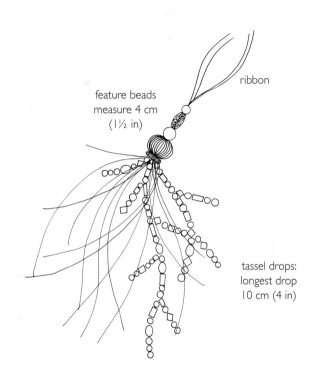

ribbon

feature beads
measure 4 cm
(1½ in)

tassel drops:
longest drop
10 cm (4 in)

$\mathcal{E}$LEGANT TASSEL

You will need

20 cm (8 in) 3 mm double-sided satin
    ribbon
5 decorative feature beads, metallic and
    coloured

1 quantity of bead mix (30–40 g) with
    larger specialty beads included
Nymo thread
beading needle

Method

Fold the ends of the ribbon over about 1 cm (¼ in) from the ends and
topstitch the folded edge together. Using a single strand of Nymo with a
double knot threaded through the folds at the base of the ribbon, begin
to randomly thread beads from the mix, beginning with small beads, until
the strand of beads is 12 cm (4½ in) long. Note thread path for top-drilled
specialty beads (see diagram on page 14).

Complete five drops in this manner and length. Create another six drops
approximately 7 cm (2½ in) long, once again beginning each drop with the
smaller beads and finishing with a feature bead, either top-drilled or centre-
drilled. Use any remaining small and medium beads to create a skirt of drops
no longer than 3.5–4 cm (1½ in) around the top of the tassel, ten drops in
total.

Fasten thread. Use a short length of thread to pull the ribbon loop through
the feature beads to form the tassel top. A knot in the ribbon or a small amount
of PVA or craft glue under the top feature bead will prevent the beads from
slipping off the ribbon.

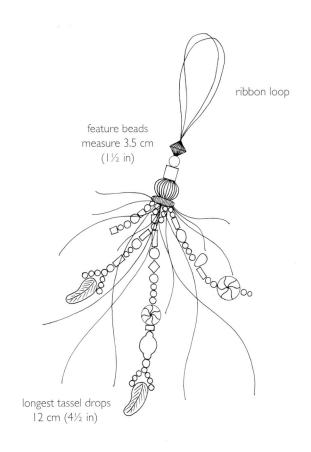

ribbon loop

feature beads
measure 3.5 cm
(1½ in)

longest tassel drops
12 cm (4½ in)

DAISY DROPS TASSEL

20 cm (8 in) 3 mm double-sided satin ribbon

4 decorative feature beads, metallic and coloured

23 acrylic flower beads in assorted pastel colours

23 x 3 mm acrylic white pearls

20 g size 12 silver-lined glass seed beads

Nymo thread

beading needle

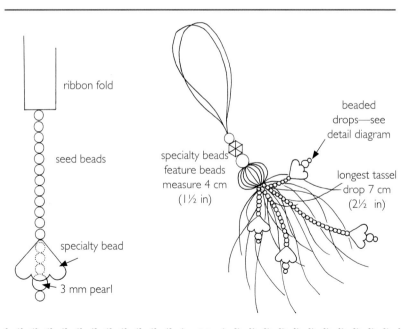

ribbon fold

seed beads

specialty beads
feature beads
measure 4 cm
(1½ in)

specialty bead

3 mm pearl

beaded drops—see detail diagram

longest tassel drop 7 cm (2½ in)

Method

Fold the ends of the ribbon over about 1 cm (¼ in) from the ends and topstitch the folded edges together. Secure a thread to the base of the ribbon.

The tassel skirt contains 23 drops of assorted lengths. Each drop is finished with a flower bead, three silver-lined glass seed beads and a 3 mm pearl, and a silver-lined glass seed bead forms the keeper bead. See diagram of thread path detail.

The drops vary in length, the longest being 7 cm (2½ in) in total and the shortest 1.5 cm (½ in) in total. Take needle and thread around the keeper bead and return through the thread path to the base of the ribbon.

WILD ORCHID TASSEL

You will need

20 cm (8 in) 3 mm double-sided satin
    ribbon
3 acrylic orchid beads
9 acrylic labellum beads
20 g size 12 silver-lined glass seed beads
21 x 3 mm cream pearls

11 x 6 mm coloured pearls to tone with
    orchid flowers
6 decorative feature beads
    (includes 2 x 6 mm coloured pearls)
Nymo thread
beading needle

Method

Fold the ends of the ribbon over about 1 cm (¼ in) from the ends and topstitch the folded edges together. Secure a thread to the base of the ribbon.

Drop A: ★8 seed beads, 1 x 3 mm pearl★, repeat from ★ to ★ 4 times, thread the needle and thread through a labellum bead from the top, 5 seed beads, 1 x 6 mm coloured pearl, 1 seed bead as the keeper bead. Take needle and thread around the keeper bead and return through the thread path to the base of the ribbon. Secure.

Drop B: as for drop A, but one beading sequence (8 seed beads, 1 x 3 mm pearl) shorter. Repeat to create 2 x drop B.

Drop C: as for drop A, but two beading sequences (8 seed beads, 1 x 3 mm pearl) shorter. Repeat to create 2 x drop C.

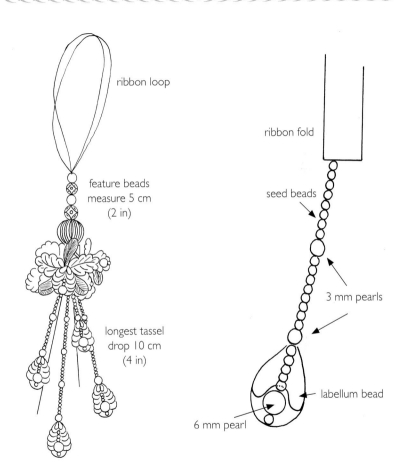

ribbon loop

feature beads
measure 5 cm
(2 in)

longest tassel
drop 10 cm
(4 in)

ribbon fold

seed beads

3 mm pearls

labellum bead

6 mm pearl

Drop D: as for A, but three beading sequences (8 seed beads, 1 x 3 mm pearl) shorter.

You will have six beaded drops attached to the ribbon.

Flower drops: Secure the thread at the ribbon base in such a position that the flower drop will sit outside the drops already made. Take the needle and thread through a flower bead from the back; pick up a labellum bead, 5 seed beads, 1 x 6 mm coloured pearl and 1 seed bead as a keeper bead. Take needle and thread around the keeper bead and return through the thread path to the base of the ribbon. Secure. Repeat for the remaining orchid flowers, three in total. Fasten thread.

Use a short length of thread to pull the ribbon loop through the feature beads to form the tassel top. A knot in the ribbon or a small amount of PVA or craft glue under the top feature bead will prevent the beads from slipping off the ribbon.

ANTIQUE PEARL TASSEL

You will need

20 cm (8 in) 7 mm silk ribbon
1 x 20 cm faceted glass bead
2 large bead caps
1 decorative feature bead
20 g size 11 seed beads (DBR 671)
80 small cast bead caps

40 x 6 mm cream glass pearls
15 teardrop glass pearls, 6 x 9 mm
15 g x 2 mm cream glass pearls
Nymo thread
beading needle

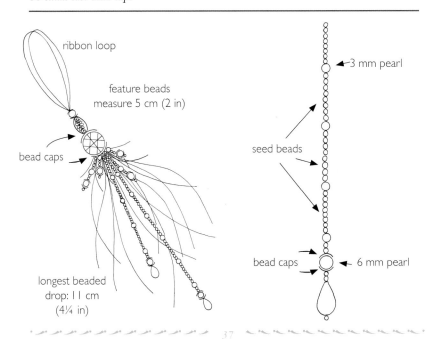

ribbon loop

feature beads
measure 5 cm (2 in)

bead caps

longest beaded
drop: 11 cm
(4¼ in)

3 mm pearl

seed beads

bead caps

6 mm pearl

Method

Fold the ends of the ribbon over about 1 cm (¼ in) from the ends and topstitch the folded edges together. Secure a thread to the base of the ribbon.

Drop A: pick up *8 seed beads, 1 x 2 mm pearl*, repeat 6 times. Pick up 2 seed beads, 1 small bead cap, 1 x 6 mm pearl, 1 small bead cap, 1 teardrop pearl and 1 seed bead, which becomes the keeper bead. Take needle and thread through the return bead path and secure to the base of the ribbon. This forms the longest drop.

Drop B: as for drop A, but removing one beading sequence (8 seed beads, 1 x 2 mm pearl). Repeat to create 2 x drop B.

Drop C: as for drop A, but removing two beading sequences (8 seed beads, 1 x 2 mm pearl). Repeat to create 2 x drop C.

Subsequent drops: continue to create shorter and shorter drops, 2 of each length, removing one more sequence each time, until there are 15 drops in total.

Skirt for tassel top

Use the following beading sequence and make the number of drops listed for each layer.

Bottom layer: 8 seed beads, 1 x 2 mm pearl, 2 seed beads, 1 small bead cap, 1 x 6 mm pearl, 1 small bead cap, 1 seed bead as keeper bead. Make 10 drops.

Middle layer: 4 seed beads, 1 x 2 mm pearl, 2 seed beads, 1 small bead cap, 1 x 6 mm pearl, 1 small bead cap, 1 seed bead as keeper bead. Make 6 drops.

Top layer: 1 x 2 mm pearl, 2 seed beads, 1 small bead cap, 1 x 6 mm pearl, 1 small bead cap, 1 seed bead as keeper bead. Make 7 drops.

Fasten thread. Use a short length of thread to pull the ribbon loop through the feature beads to form the tassel top. A knot in the ribbon or a small amount of PVA or craft glue under the top feature bead will prevent the beads from slipping off the ribbon.

$\mathcal{T}$EARDROP TASSEL

This tassel combines bead tassel and bead crusting techniques, and also requires you to wrap a large wooden bead in ribbon, a technique described later in the book.

You will need

2 m (1¼ yd) x 3 mm double-sided satin ribbon

60 g Czech glass bead mix: this includes a variety of shapes and sizes, usually in complementary or toning colours, and specialty beads in a variety of finishes

30 g size 11 seed beads to tone with Czech mix

15 g x 6 mm bugle beads

60 Swarovski 4 mm bicones

50 x 6 mm glass bicones

1 x 20 mm raw wooden bead

5 feature beads

Nymo thread

beading needle

Method

Cut 20 cm (8 in) of double-sided satin ribbon and set aside for the tassel loop. Using the remaining ribbon, cover the wooden bead by threading the ribbon through the centre hole and overlapping the wraps as you work around the bead. Secure the end of the ribbon. See diagram and detailed instructions on page 51.

See diagram for bead crusting on page 48.

Sew one end of the reserved 20 cm (8 in) of ribbon to one side of the opening at the 'top' of the wooden bead and the other end to the opposite side. This creates the loop at the top of the tassel.

The drops for this tassel are sewn to this ribbon-covered wooden bead, beginning with the longest drop sewn at the base of the bead. Seed beads, bugle beads and the occasional Swarovski crystal or glass bicone create the main length of the drop before the specialty bead is added, for a total length of 8 cm from the base of the bead. Drops of ever-decreasing lengths are sewn to the bead as you work over the surface, approximately 3 mm apart. Specialty beads and crystals are only added at the end of each drop.

Ensure as you stitch that the drops are created shorter as you move up the bead, otherwise the longer drops will cover and disguise previous drops. Tension each drop and hold the bead up as you add each one to ensure they are the required length. Once the bead is covered the last layer of drops is stitched in place. These are formed with 2 or 3 seed beads and a specialty bead sewn to the rim of the ribbon-covered hole in the wooden bead. Fasten thread. Use a short length of thread to pull the ribbon loop through the feature beads to form the tassel top. A knot in the ribbon or a small amount of PVA or craft glue under the top feature bead will prevent the beads from slipping off the ribbon.

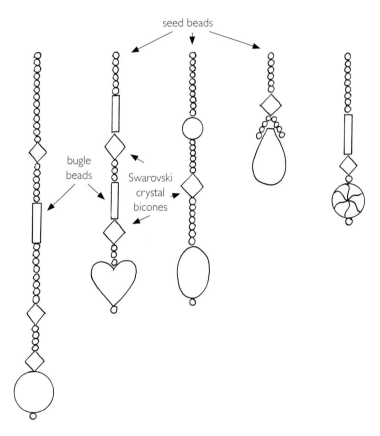

seed beads

bugle beads

Swarovski crystal bicones

Examples of drops for the teardrop tassel. Feature beads measure 5.5 cm (2¼ in), and the longest drop measures 10 cm (4 in).

Traveller's Tassel

The beads I used for my Traveller's Tassel were bought on various overseas teaching trips. They took up minimal room in my luggage and when designed into this tassel allowed me to create a unique souvenir of my trips. I still recall where most of the beads were bought and had fun threading them one creative evening.

You will need

30 cm (12 in) x 1 cm double-sided satin ribbon

3 decorative silver beads

assorted sterling silver, glass and crystal beads in various sizes, shapes and finishes

spacer beads and bead caps in various sizes and styles

20 g size 12 seed beads in toning colour to act as additional spacers

Nymo thread

beading needle

Method

Fold the ends of the ribbon over about 1 cm (¼ in) from the ends and topstitch the folded edges together. Secure a thread to the base of the ribbon.

Begin each drop by picking up 12 seed beads before randomly attaching the beads to each drop. The very decorative nature of this tassel encourages the generous inclusion of bead caps and spacer beads, and the repetition of bead patterns either side of individual beads. The larger specialty beads are used at the base of each drop, which gives consistency to the overall design.

Each drop, and there are twelve of them, is approximately 15 cm (6 in) long. If the range of beads used in this tassel is a little overwhelming you may try a similar one but make each of the twelve drops the same. Fasten thread.

Use a short length of thread to pull the ribbon loop through the feature beads to form the tassel top. A knot in the ribbon or a small amount of PVA or craft glue under the top feature bead will prevent the beads from slipping off the ribbon.

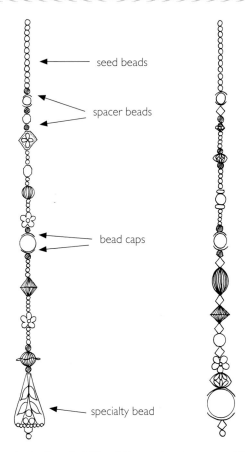

seed beads

spacer beads

bead caps

specialty bead

Detail of typical drop in the Traveller's Tassel. Feature beads measure 5.5 cm (2¼ in);
the longest drop measures 15 cm (6 in).

Bead Crusting

CONSTRUCTION BASICS

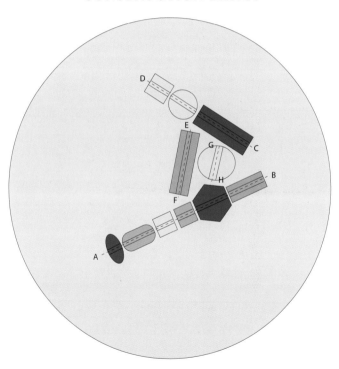

* The materials listed for each item will create one crusted item as shown.

* Nymo beading thread used for all projects.

* When sewing the crusting beads in place, always take a stitch in the
  fabric or ribbon base that is equal to or slightly longer than the space
  taken up on the needle by the beads that are to be sewn into place.
  By stitching the beads in this manner you will ensure that they lie flat
  against the surface and there will be no loops in the bead strand. If the
  bead strand does not sit as flat as you would like, a couching stitch across
  the middle will encourage the beads to lie flat.

* Always use a ribbon or fabric which is similar in colour to the selected
  bead mix to ensure that any small spaces between the beads will become
  almost invisible when the item is crusted.

CRUSTED TASSEL

You will need

1 raw wooden bead 25 mm (1 in)
  diameter
30 g bead mix in the colour of your
  choice—see notes on bead mixes
2 m (2½ yd) x 3 mm double-sided satin
  ribbon

3 feature beads
2 skeins Rajmahal stranded art silk
  thread, colour to complement bead
  mix
Nymo thread
beading needle

ribbon loop

feature beads

crusted bead

tassel skirt

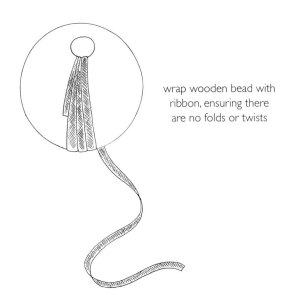

wrap wooden bead with
ribbon, ensuring there
are no folds or twists

Method

Cut 30 cm (12 in) of ribbon and set aside for the tassel loop.

Using the remaining ribbon, wrap the wooden bead to completely cover the surface and give a solid base on which to stitch the beads. Overlap the second wrap to hold the beginning of the ribbon in place and stitch the end of the ribbon to the previous wrap to secure. The ribbon should not have any twists as you cover the bead, both inside the centre hole and around the outside of the bead.

Using a single strand of Nymo thread, commence stitching the beads to the ribbon base you have created. You can place 2–6 beads at a time, depending on their size. Work randomly around the curved surface. As you work fill any smaller spaces with one or two beads sewn in the same manner until the surface is tightly 'crusted'.

Take the wrappers off the two skeins of thread, but do not cut the knot holding the ends together. Working with one skein of thread at a time, make three equal loops from the circle of thread. Use a doubled length of Nymo thread to sew these loops together firmly at the point opposite to where the ends are knotted together. Repeat with the other skein of thread. Butt the sewn ends together and neatly stitch together.

Securely stitch the cut ends of the reserved 20 cm (8 in) of ribbon to the sewn-together bundle of thread. Ensure the thread bundle hangs directly below the ribbon loop. Use a short length of thread to pull the ribbon loop through the crusted bead and the feature beads to form the tassel top. Pull this thread until the sewn loops of the skeins of thread disappear inside the crusted bead.

A knot in the ribbon or a small amount of PVA or craft glue under the top feature bead will prevent the beads from slipping off the ribbon. Cut the thread loops apart at the base of the tassel and use an old toothbrush to gently tease these threads apart. Steam to straighten.

$\mathscr{T}$INY CRUSTED TASSEL

This tassel is a smaller version of the Crusted Tassel above. The construction technique is the same, apart from the variations noted under Method.

You will need

1 raw wooden bead 16 mm in diameter

25 g bead mix in the colour of your choice (see notes on bead mixes)

1.5 m (1¾ yd) 3 mm double-sided satin ribbon

3 feature beads

1 skein Rajmahal stranded art silk thread, colour to complement bead mix

Nymo thread

Beading needle

Method variations

Cut 25 cm (10 in) of ribbon and set aside for tassel loop.

Fold the skein of thread into five loops and secure.

CRUSTED BAUBLE

You will need

1 raw wooden bead 25 mm diameter
30 g bead mix in the colour of your
   choice (see notes on bead mixes)
2 m (2½ yd) 3 mm double-sided satin
   ribbon

3 feature beads
Nymo thread
beading needle

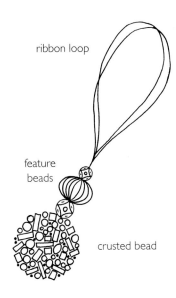

ribbon loop

feature
beads

crusted bead

Method

Cut 30 cm (12 in) from the ribbon and set aside for tassel loop.

Using the remaining ribbon, wrap the wooden bead to completely cover the surface and give a solid base on which to stitch the beads. See diagram and instructions on page 51.

Sew one end of the reserved 20 cm (8 in) of ribbon to one side of the opening at the 'top' of the wooden bead and the other end to the opposite side. This creates the loop at the top of the tassel.

Using a single strand of Nymo thread, commence stitching the beads to the ribbon base you have created. You can place 2–6 beads at a time, depending on their size. Work randomly around the curved surface. As you work, fill any smaller spaces with one or two beads sewn in the same manner until the surface is tightly 'crusted'.

Use a short length of thread to pull the ribbon loop through the feature beads to form the tassel top. A knot in the ribbon or a small amount of PVA or craft glue under the top feature bead will prevent the beads from slipping off the ribbon.

CRUSTED PRISM

You will need

1 raw wooden bead 20 mm in diameter
25 g bead mix in the colour of your
    choice (see notes on bead mixes)
1.5 m (1¾ yd) 3 mm double-sided satin
    ribbon

4 feature beads, 2 faceted, 2 metallic
1 cone-shaped bead cap
1 faceted clear drop
Nymo thread
beading needle

Method

Cut 30 cm (12 in) from the length of ribbon and set aside for tassel loop.

Sew the two ends of the ribbon together to form a loop, set aside.

Using the remaining ribbon, wrap the wooden bead to completely cover the surface and give a solid base on which to stitch the beads. See diagram and instructions on page 51.

Using a single strand of Nymo thread, commence stitching the beads to the ribbon base you have created. You can place 2–6 beads at a time, depending on their size. Work randomly around the curved surface. As you work fill any smaller spaces with one or two beads sewn in the same manner until the surface is tightly 'crusted'.

Attach a doubled length of Nymo to the base of the ribbon loop. Take this thread through the 10mm faceted feature bead, the filigree bead cap and then the faceted drop. The feature bead acts as the keeper bead. Take the thread back through the top of the filigree bead cap and the 10mm faceted bead and stitch firmly to the base of the ribbon loop.

ribbon loop

crusted bead

bead cap

faceted drop

Use a short length of thread to pull the ribbon loop through the crusted wooden bead and the remaining feature beads to form the tassel top. A knot in the ribbon or a small amount of PVA or craft glue under the top feature bead will prevent the beads from slipping off the ribbon.

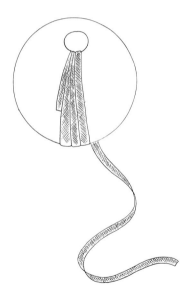

CRUSTED BOOKMARK

You will need

2 x 16 mm raw wooden beads
1.5 m (1¾ yd) 3 mm double-sided satin
    ribbon
30 cm (12 in), or length required, of
    6 mm velvet ribbon

20 g bead mix
Nymo thread
beading needle

Method

Cut the length of satin ribbon in half. Using one length of ribbon wrap one
wooden bead to completely cover the surface and give a solid base on which
to stitch the beads. See diagram and instructions on page 51.

Repeat for the second wooden bead.

Stitch the length of velvet ribbon inside the
remaining open hole of the two ribbon-covered
beads. Using a single strand of Nymo
thread, commence stitching
the beads to the ribbon
bases you have created. You
can place 2–6 beads at a
time depending on their
size. Work randomly around
the curved surface. As you work fill
any smaller spaces with one or two
beads sewn in the same manner
until the surface is tightly 'crusted'.
Secure your thread.

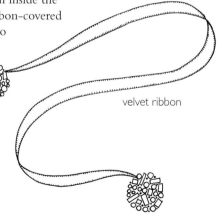

velvet ribbon

CRUSTED HAIRCLIPS AND COMBS

You will need

hairclips and combs
bias-cut fabric strip 2.5 cm (1 in) wide to
    cover the combs
1.5 m (1¾ yd) 7 mm silk ribbon to
    cover the hairclips

25 g bead mix
Nymo thread
beading needle

Method

COMB

Cut a strip of fabric 2.5 cm (1 in) longer than hair comb. Fold over the ends
and the sides about 1 cm (³/8 in). Fold the fabric strip in half again and slip
the top edge of the comb inside the fabric until it butts up against the fold.
Slip stitch the fabric together between the teeth of the comb and at both
ends. Crust the top surface tightly with the bead mix. (If a tooth of the comb
breaks through use, the stitches holding the bead-crusted fabric in place can
be snipped apart and the fabric placed over a replacement comb and slip
stitched into place.)

HAIRCLIP

Wrap the 7 mm silk ribbon firmly over the hairclip, covering the surface
completely if possible. Crust the topmost surface of the clip until the ribbon
is no longer visible.

CRUSTED BUTTONS

You will need

Clover brand button blanks with holes,
   or fabric-covered buttons to size
   requirements

25 g bead mix
Nymo thread
beading needle

Method

The Clover button
blank has a perforated
plastic top layer that
will allow you to sew
the beads directly onto
it. If you prefer to use
fabric-covered buttons,
the beads can be sewn
directly onto the fabric.

   Sew the selected
bead mix onto the
button, ensuring the
bead mix topples over
the edge of either type
of button to fully hide
the background.

CRUSTED LIDDED BOWL

You will need

stained wooden lidded bowl with centre
  recess
fabric to match colour of bead mix
  (dupion silk is ideal as it gathers
  consistently and neatly)
cardboard circle to fit neatly inside recess
  of bowl

circle of thin quilter's wadding
30 g bead mix
Nymo thread
beading needle
embroidery hoop

Method

Use the cardboard disc that fits the recess of the bowl to trace an outline on
the fabric. All the bead crusting must fall inside this outline.

Fit the fabric in the
embroidery hoop. Using a
single strand of Nymo thread,
commence stitching the beads
inside the circle you have
marked. You can place 2–6 beads
at a time depending on their
size. Work randomly over the
surface of the fabric. As you
work, fill any smaller spaces with
one or two beads sewn in the
same manner until the surface is
tightly crusted. Fasten thread.

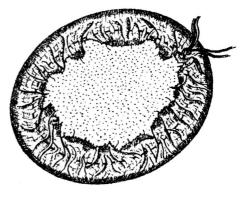

Using a doubled strand of beading thread, work a row of even tacking stitches approximately 1 cm ($^3/_8$ in) out from the edge of the circle. Leave thread ends approximately 10 cm (4 in) at the top of the work at start and finish of the tacking stitches. Trim the fabric to within 1 cm ($^3/_8$ in) of this row of tacking stitches. Place the crusted fabric face down on a flat surface. Centre the disc of wadding and the disc of cardboard over the crusted fabric. Use the ends of the tacking threads to draw the edges of the fabric around the disc of cardboard. Even out the gathers and tie the threads to secure.

Using craft glue, glue the fabric in place in the recess of the bowl.

SATIN-COVERED BOX

The satin-covered box is worked in the same manner. Trace around the removable lid to mark the boundary of the bead crusting.

$\mathcal{C}$RUSTED BROOCH

You will need

wooden brooch with centre recess
fabric to match colour of bead mix
    (dupion silk is ideal as it gathers
    consistently and neatly)
cardboard circle to fit neatly inside recess
    of brooch

circle of thin quilter's wadding
15 g bead mix
Nymo thread
beading needle
embroidery hoop

Method

The brooch is worked in
a similar manner to the
Lidded Bowl above. Ensure
the cardboard disc fits
inside the recess neatly and
that any crusting remains
inside the boundary marked
on the fabric.

CRUSTED PAPERWEIGHT

You will need

thin craft cardboard
heavy filling to weight the object, e.g.
    small lead sinkers, rice, sand
silk dupion

15 g bead mix
glue stick
Nymo thread
beading needle

paperweight
pattern (50%)

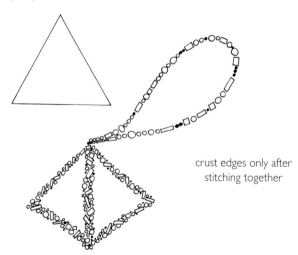

crust edges only after
stitching together

Method

Cut 4 triangles using the cardboard pattern. Cut 4 triangles of silk 6 mm (¼ in) larger all round than the cardboard triangles. Using the glue stick, carefully cover the triangles with the silk, wrapping the excess fabric over the edges and glueing in place on the back of the triangles. Top stitch the edges of three triangles together. Fill with selected weight and top stitch the remaining triangle in place. Crust all edges of the triangle to camouflage the stitching to a width of 6–8 mm (¼ in). Finish off.

Firmly attach a length of Nymo thread to one corner of the weight. Thread approximately 15 cm (6 in) of the crusting mix onto the thread and sew to the same corner to form a lifting loop. Fasten off thread.

CRUSTED PINCUSHION

You will need

30 cm (12 in) square of fabric (I used
    moiré taffeta)
30 g bead mix to complement the fabric
Rajmahal stranded art silk thread or
    ribbon in colour to complement the
    fabric

2 decorative metallic beads
1 button to match colour of fabric
sewing machine, matching cotton, toy
    filling or stuffing

Method

Cut four 15 cm (6 in) squares of fabric. With right sides together, sew around
pairs of squares to make two squares of double thickness, using a 6 mm (¼ in)
seam allowance and leaving a 5 cm (2 in) gap along one edge only of each
square to turn through to the right side. Turn through, press and slip stitch
the openings closed. Squares must be exactly the same size when complete.

Place a pin at the midpoint of each side of one square. Using a double
length of sewing cotton, butt the corner of the other square to the marked
midpoint of the first square, as shown on the diagram on page 79, and whip
stitch the two sides together as shown on the diagram. Continue around the
cushion until seven sides have been joined. Tightly fill with toy fill, and then
whip stitch the last seam closed. Using a beading needle and a single strand
of thread, crust the sewn edge to a width of 6–8 mm (¼ in). Make a twisted
cord from the Rajmahal thread, or use a loop of ribbon, to make a lifting

loop. Sew this in place through the middle of the pincushion to the button at the centre base. Use a short length of thread to pull the ribbon or cord loop through the feature beads to form the lifting loop. A small amount of PVA or craft glue under the top feature bead will prevent the beads from slipping off the ribbon.

pincushion pattern
enlarge at 140%

6 mm (¼ in) seam allowance included

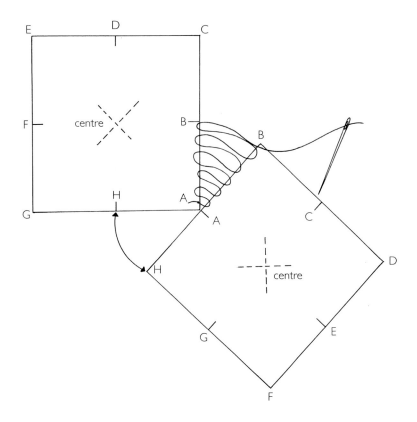